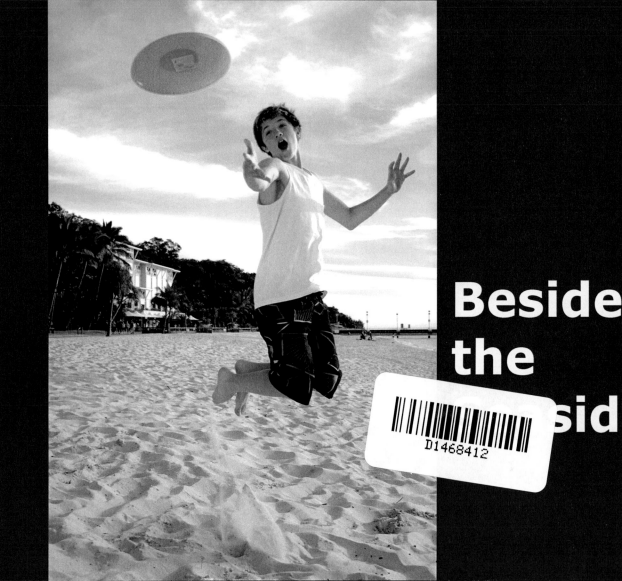

Beside
the
sid

A storytelling book about the regular or holiday experience of walking along the seashore. Images portray some of the things, views or people we may see, such as children playing. To support reminiscence and recognition some step-by-step images are presented for selected beach activities.

This book is an interactive activity for a carer or therapist to share with a person in care in one-to-one situations or as a group activity. It is designed for people with Alzheimer's disease, dementia, memory loss and frail aged persons. The images are intended to faciltate social identity and memory stimulation through recognition of the familiar.

Carers' Viewing Suggestions:

. Sit beside your care-recipient in a non-invasive position, express your interest & respond to care-recipient's engagement.
. View the book with your care-recipient in a quiet area with no distracting noises or activities nearby.
· Make sure there are no bright lights or bright windows to the viewer's side or in front, as these will be distracting.
· Make sure there are no shadows or reflecting lights falling on the pages.
· Provide focus by avoiding distracting patterns within the viewing area. If sitting at a table place a plain cloth (not bright, fluro or white) over fabric patterns, clutter or other activity resources.
. Provide a plain covered pillow or cushion on your care-recipient's lap to support their hands and the book.
. Check that care-recipients glasses are clean.
. Where possible allow your care-recipient control of turning the pages and pausing for engagement and reminiscence.
. Make a note of interesting stories or memories that your reader has talked about or images that attracted attention for future interaction.
. A sigh, nod, smile or other non-verbal expression may be considered as social interaction for some persons in care.

www.sharetimepictures.com.au

Photography, Paintings & Design: Judi Parkinson B.V.A, F.A., B.A. (Psychology), M.A. (Hons) V.A.

Parkinson, Judi, 1948-
Beside the Seaside - A Share-Time Picture Book for Reminiscing and Storytelling
Publisher: Brisbane, Judi Parkinson for Share-Time Pictures, Amazon Edition 2015
ISBN-13: 978-1512164411 - ISBN-10: 1512164410
Series: Non-Verbal Reminiscent Books for People with Alzheimer's disease, Dementia and Memory Loss - Volume 6

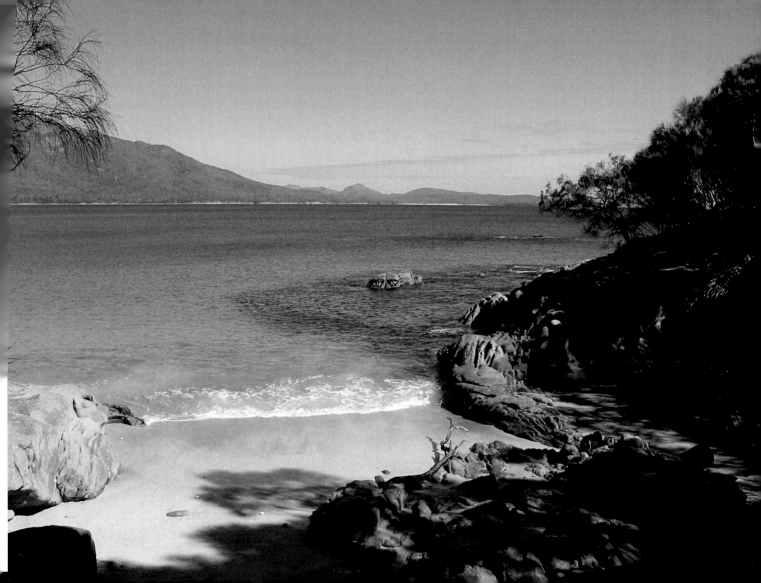

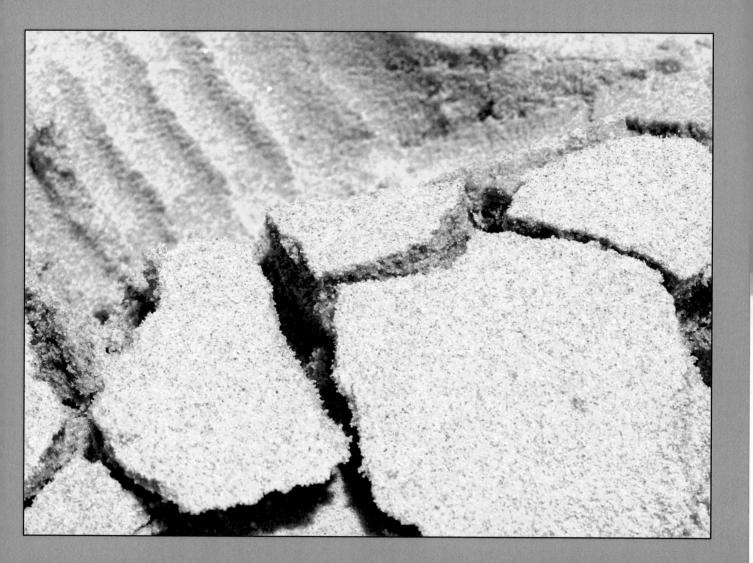

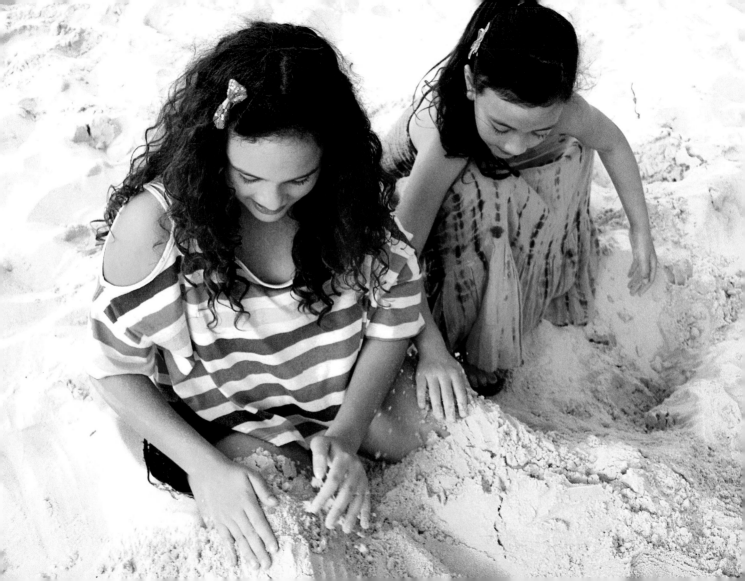

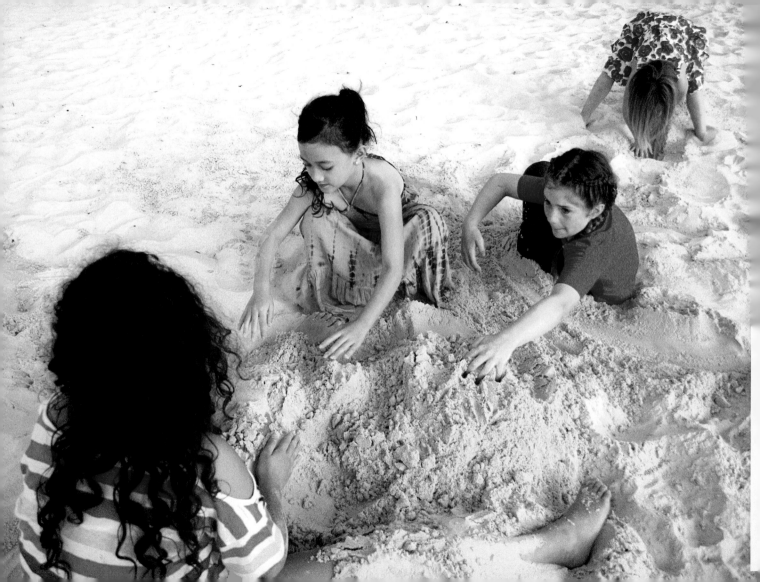

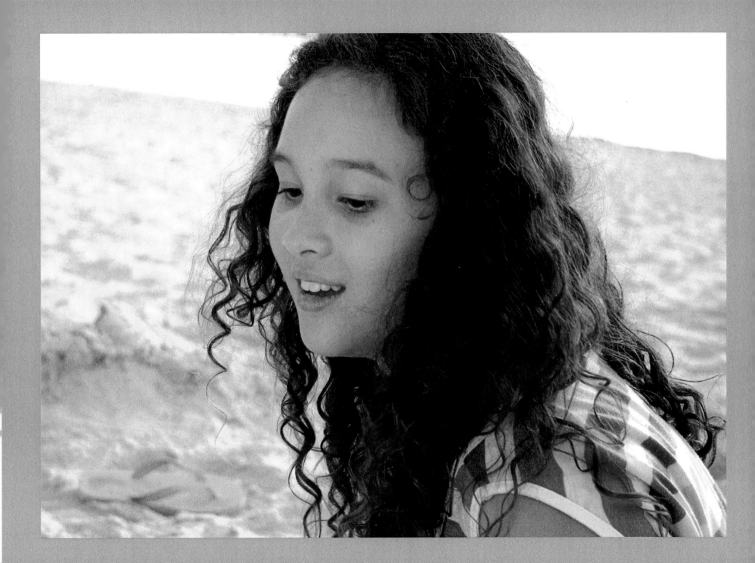

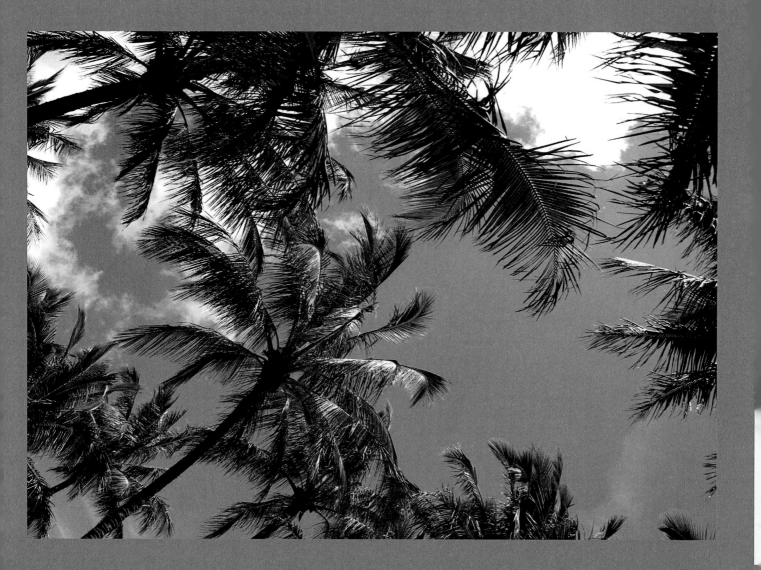

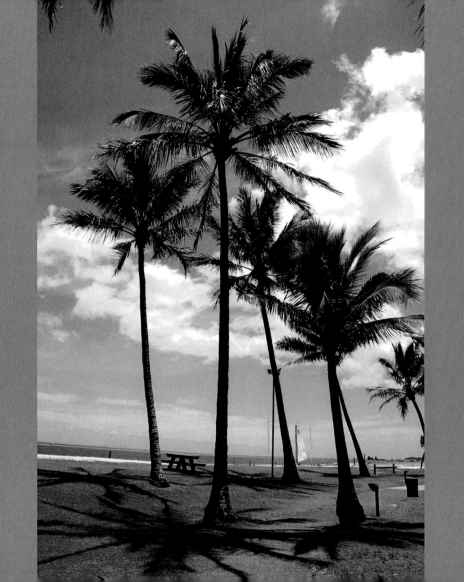

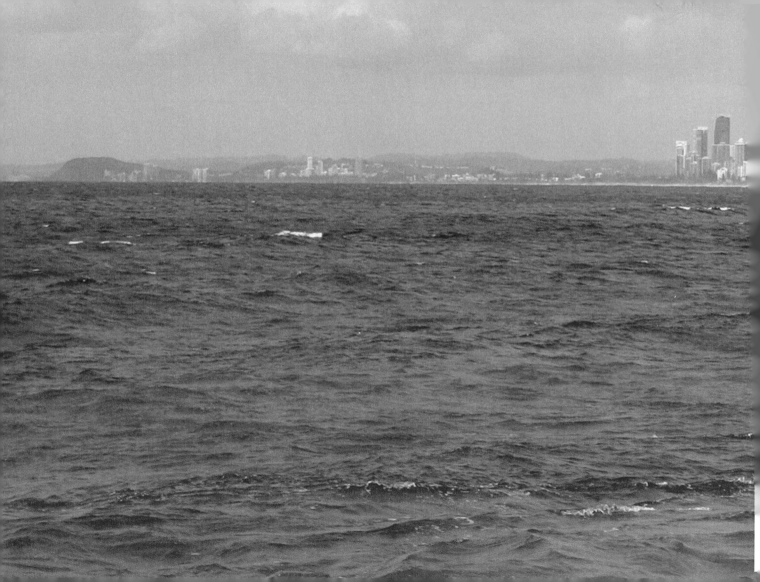

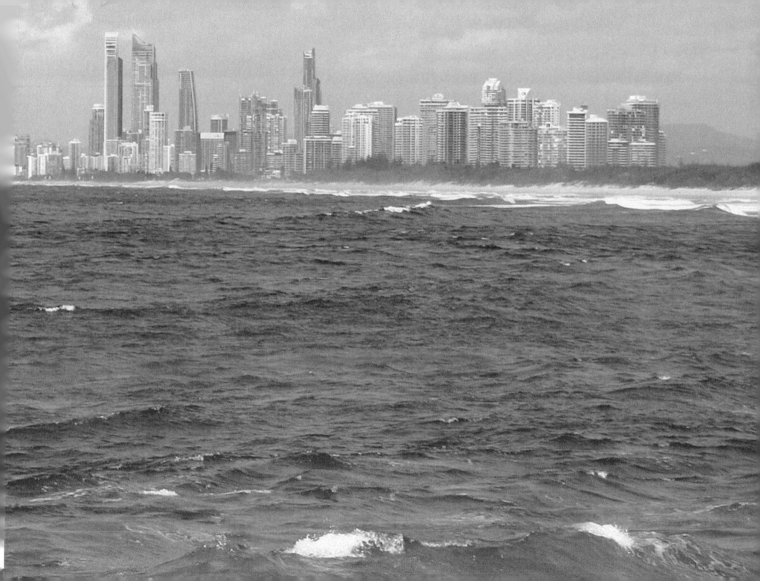

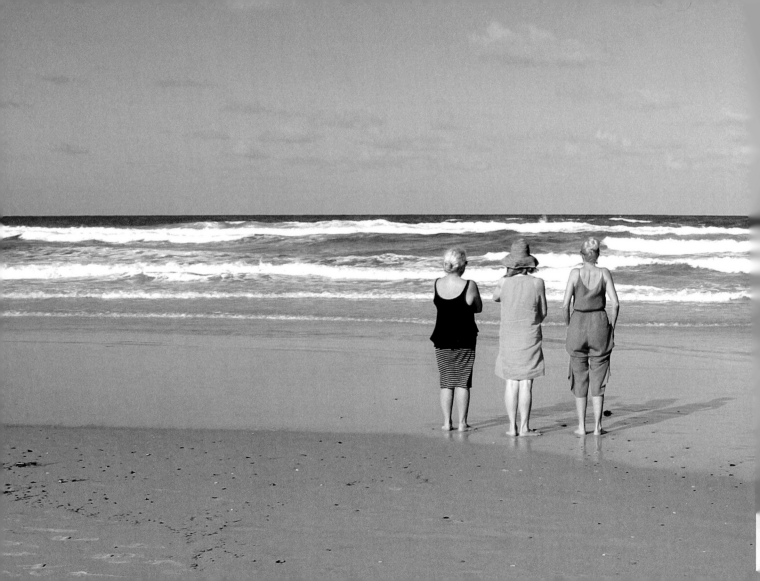

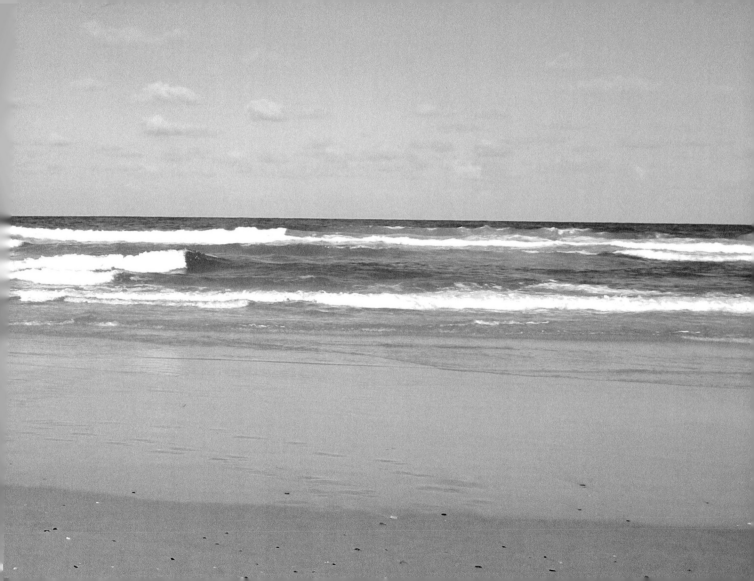

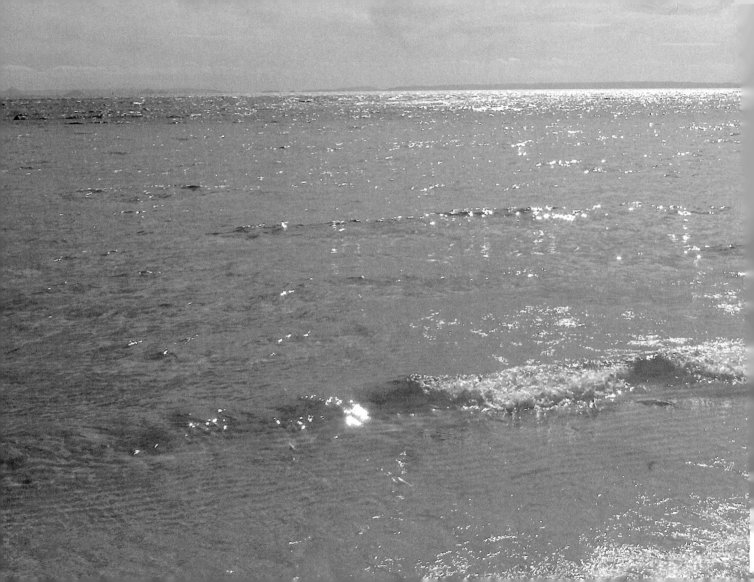

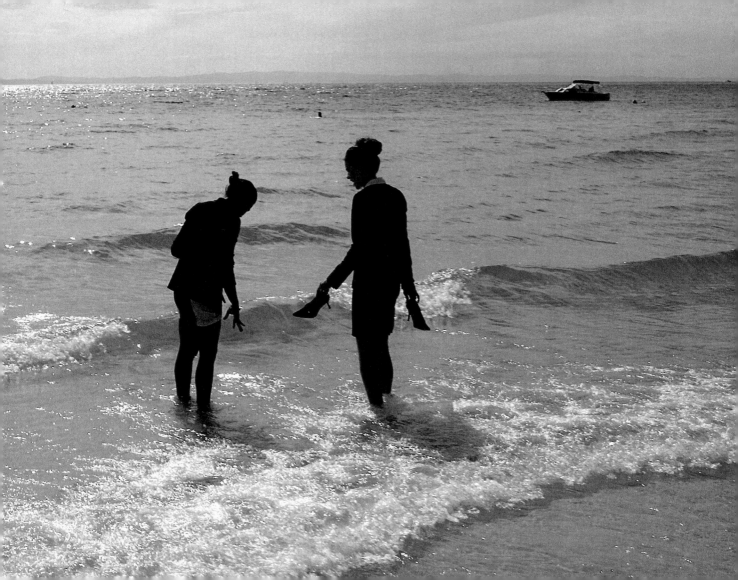

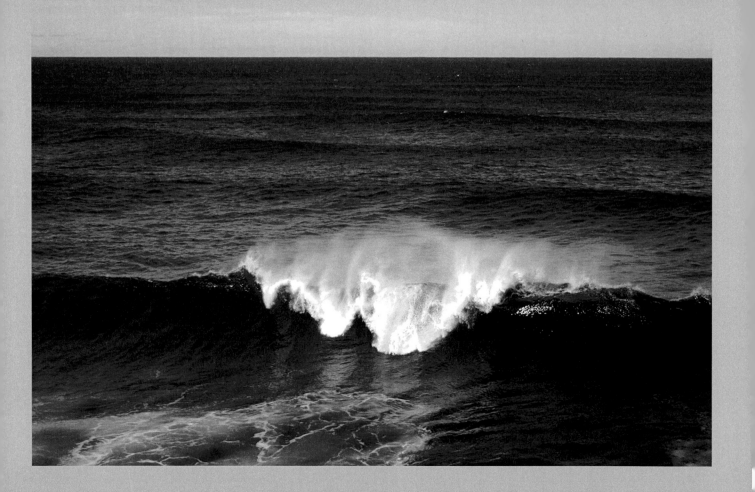

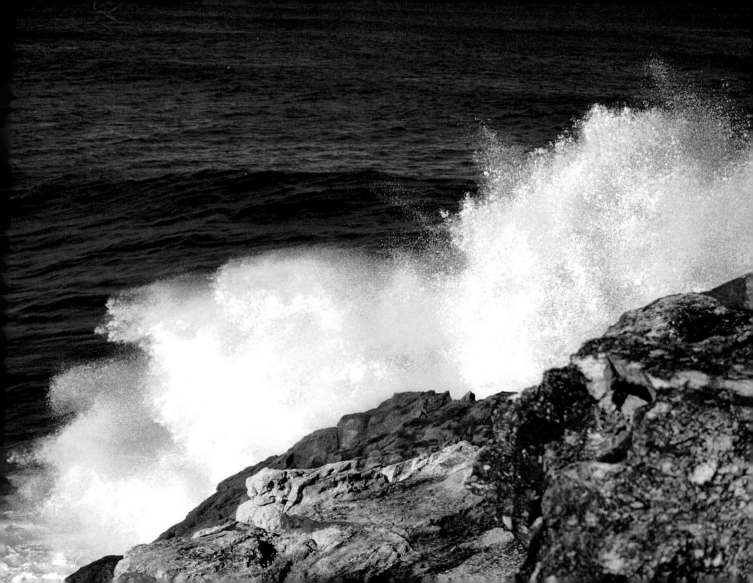

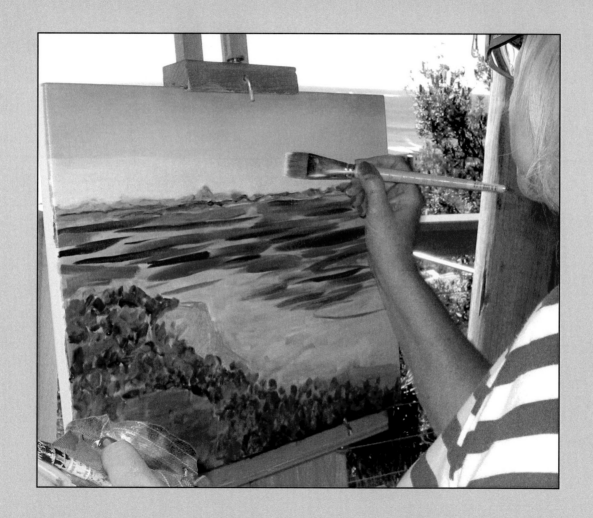

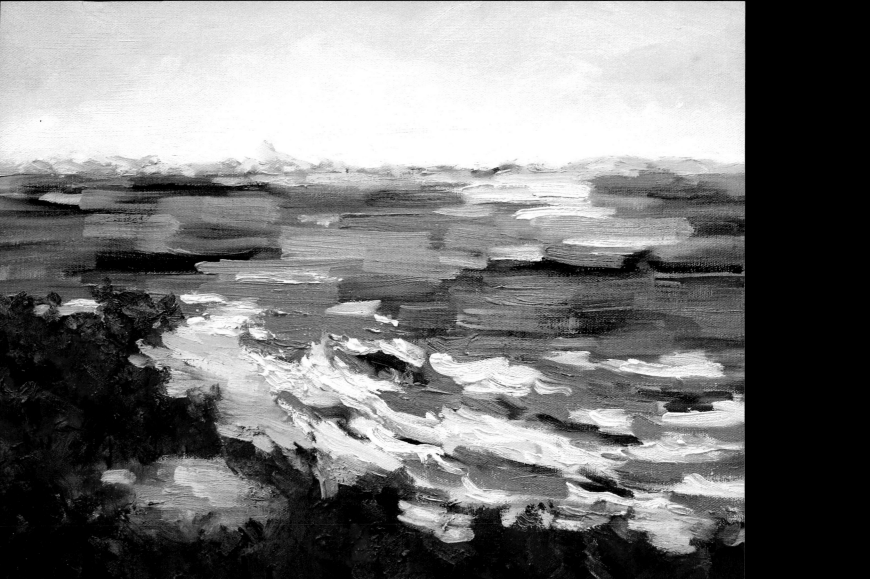

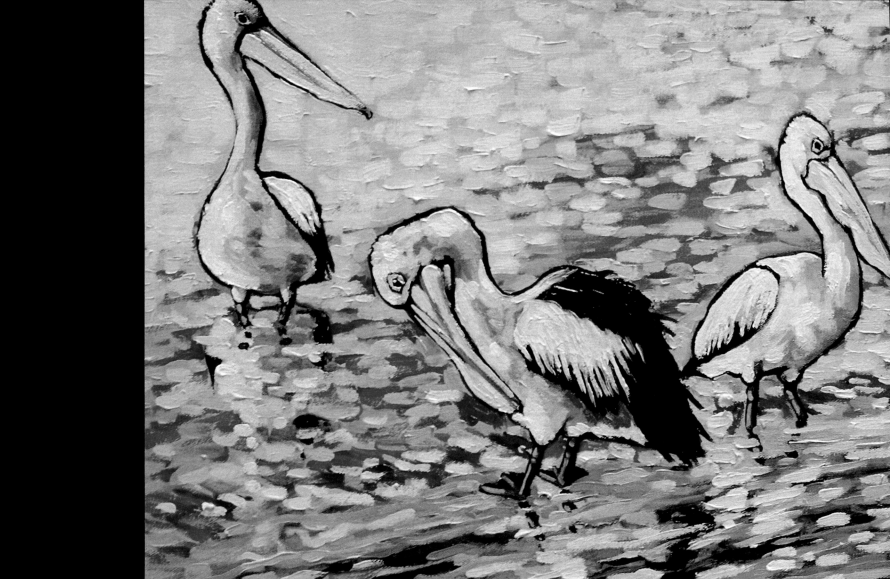

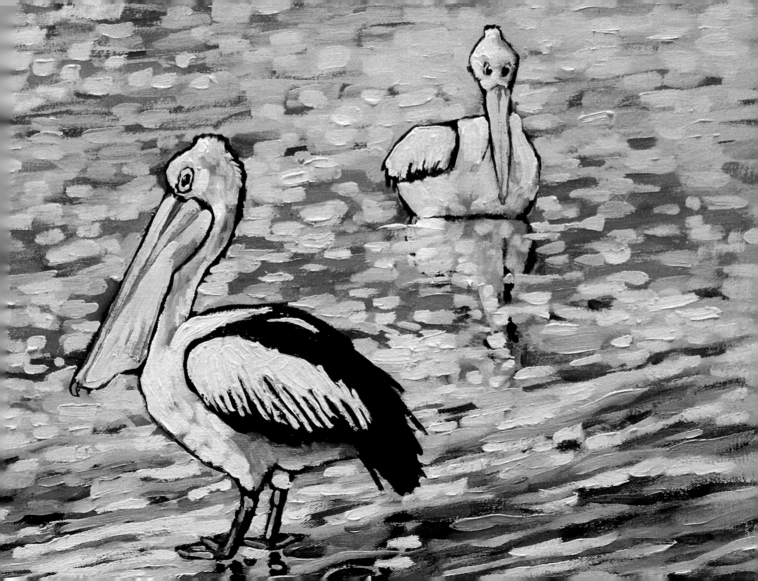

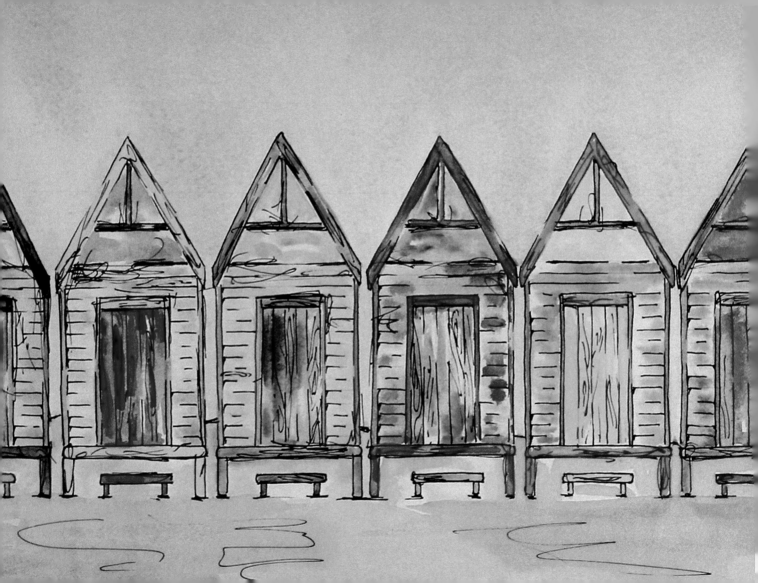

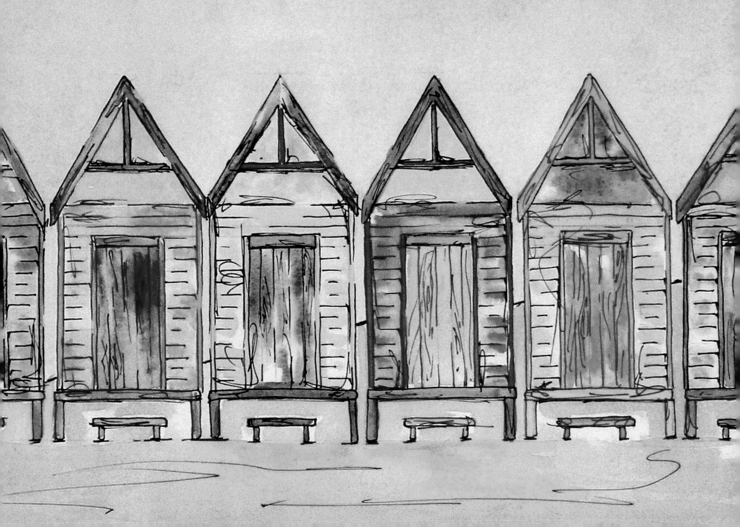

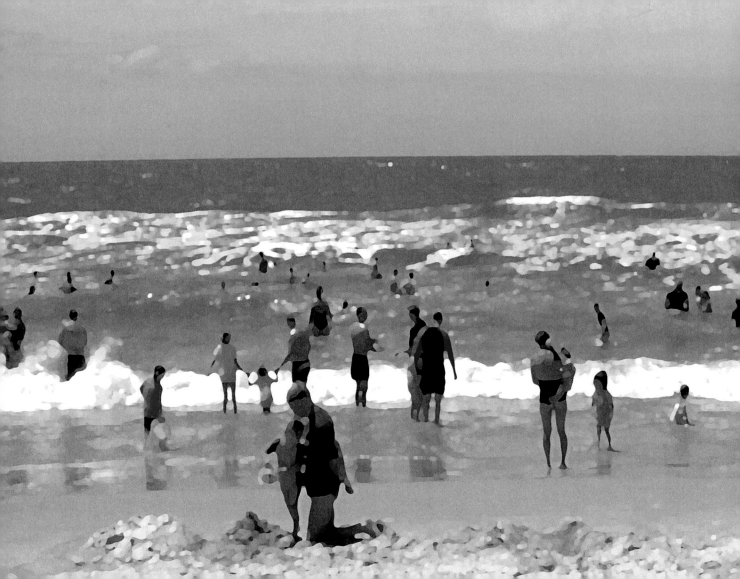

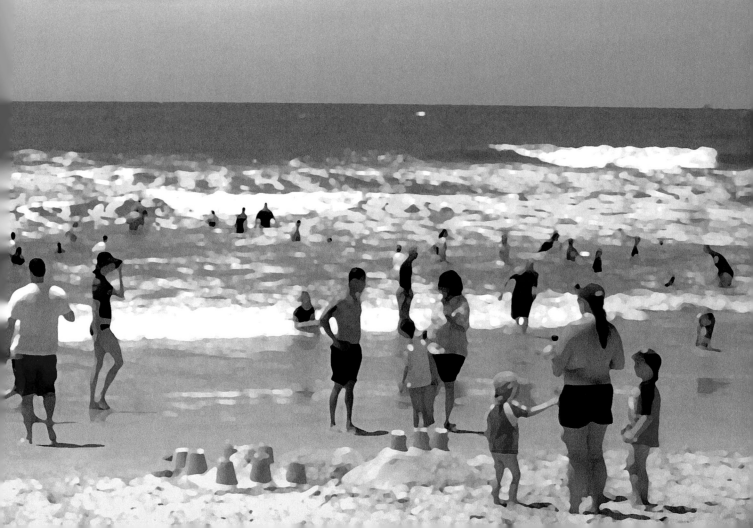

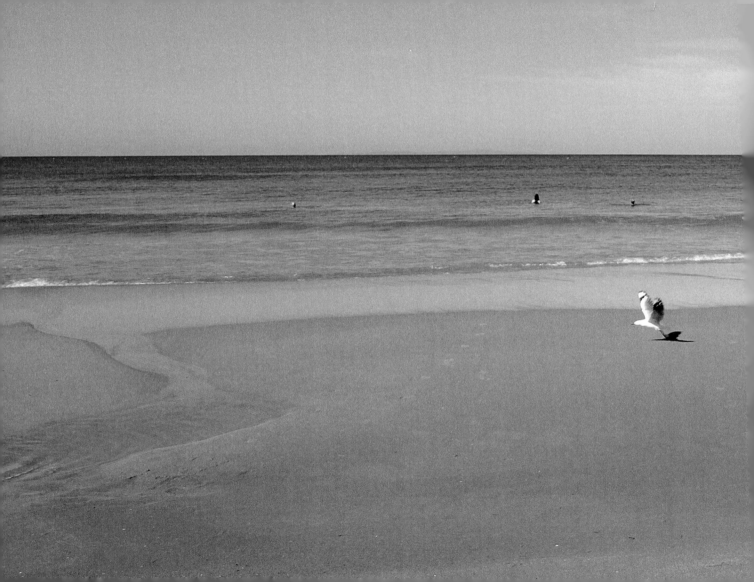

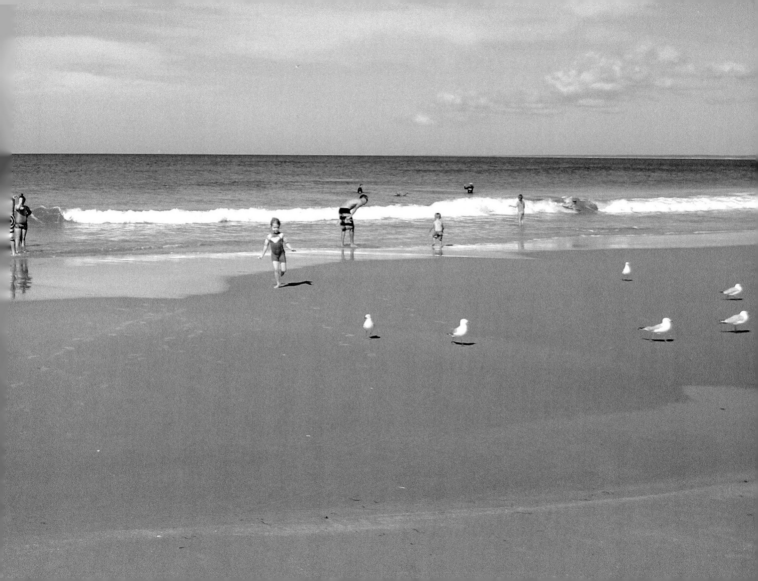

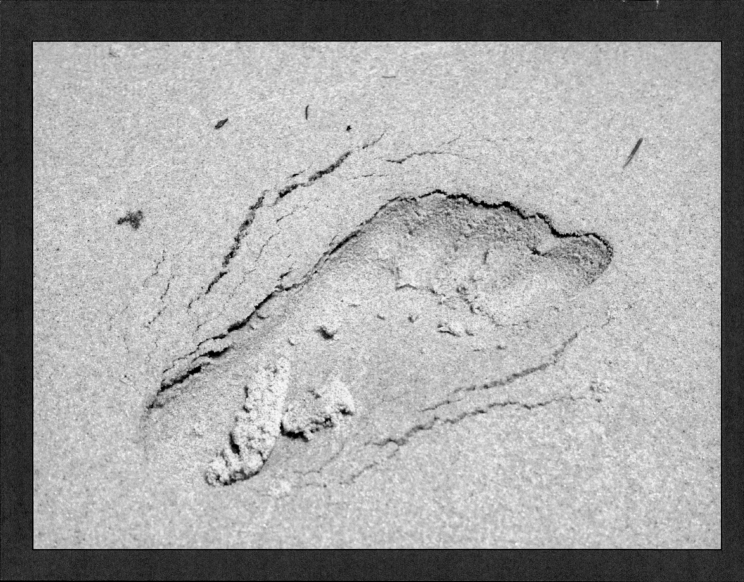

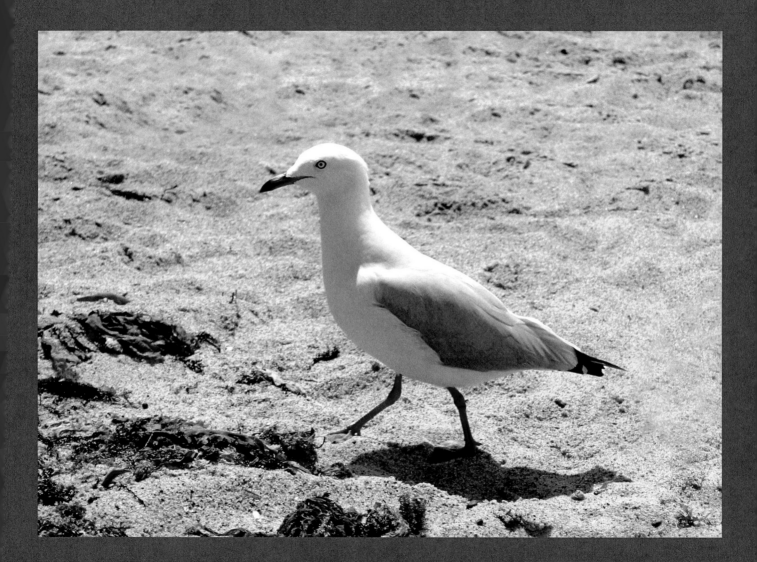

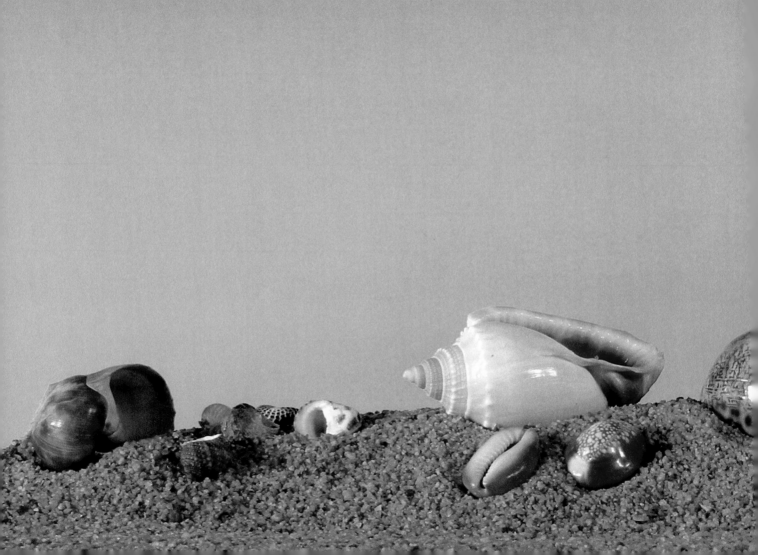

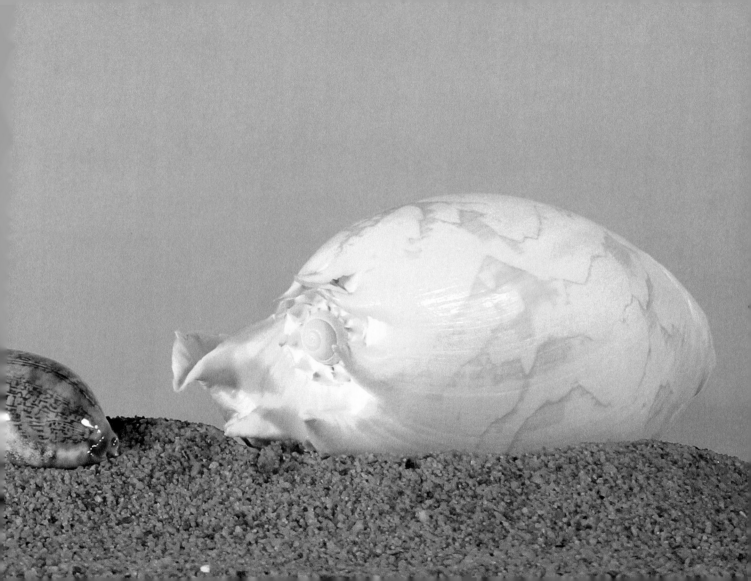

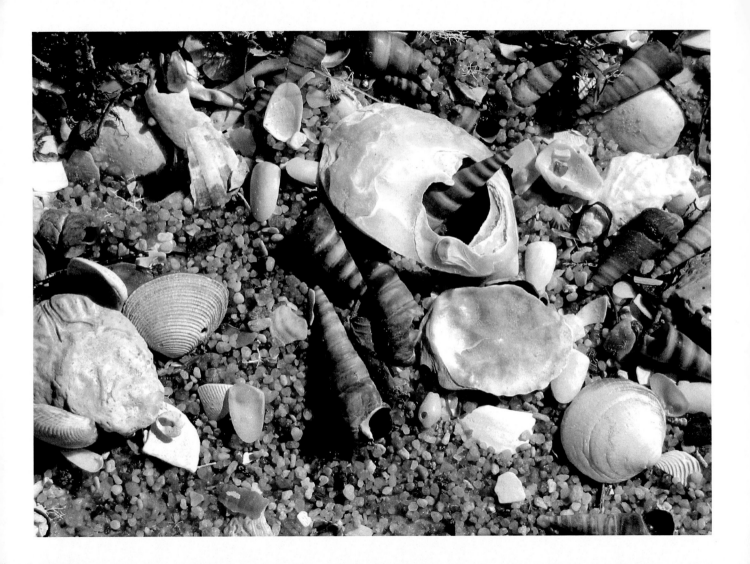

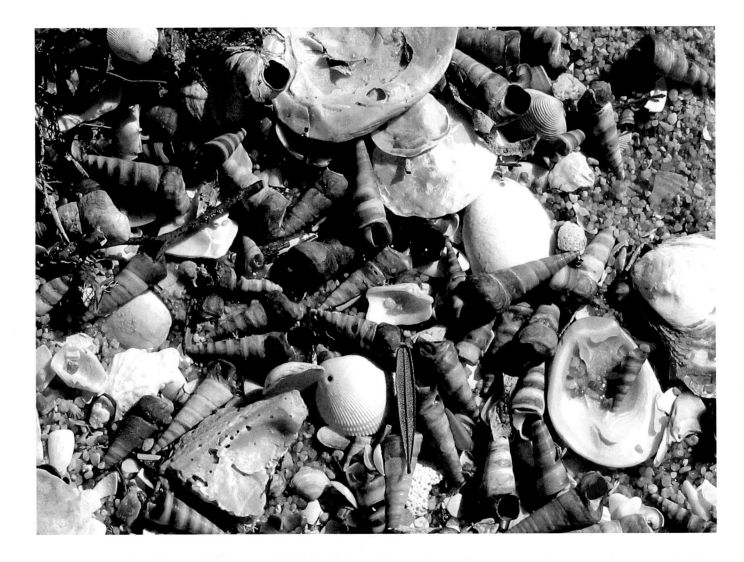

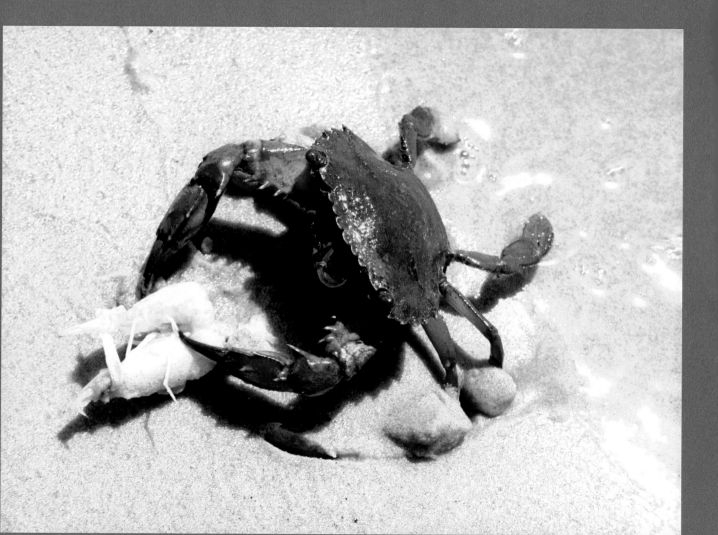

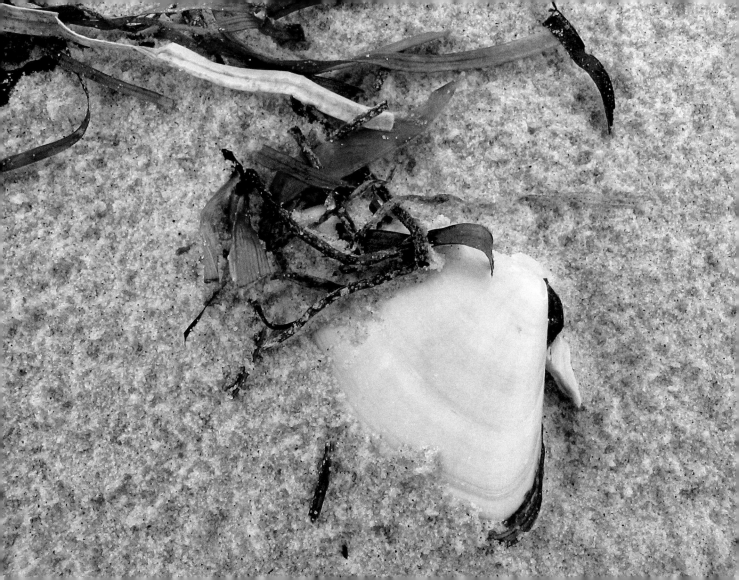

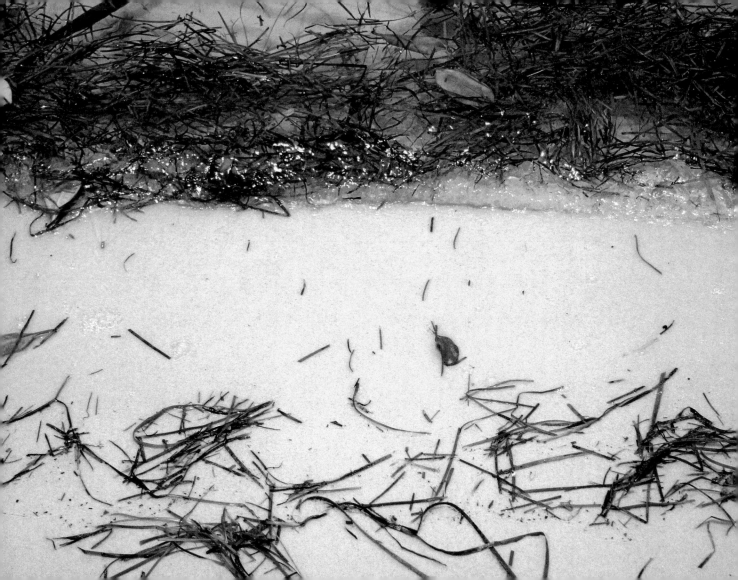

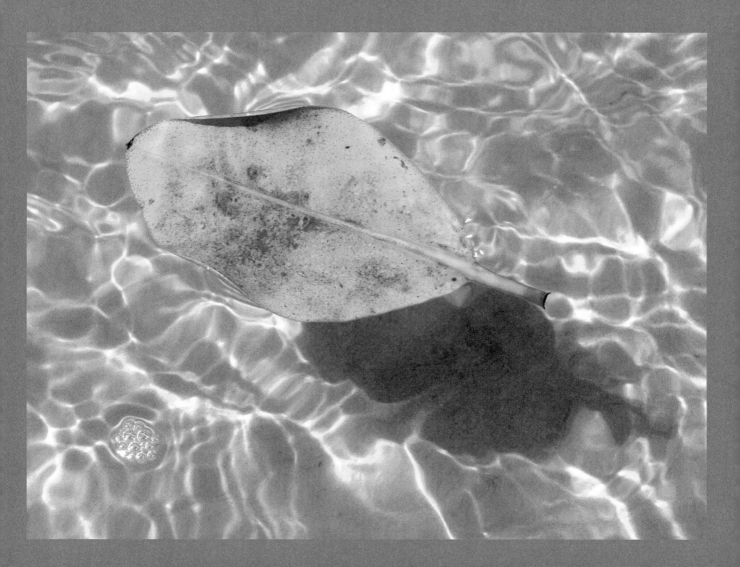

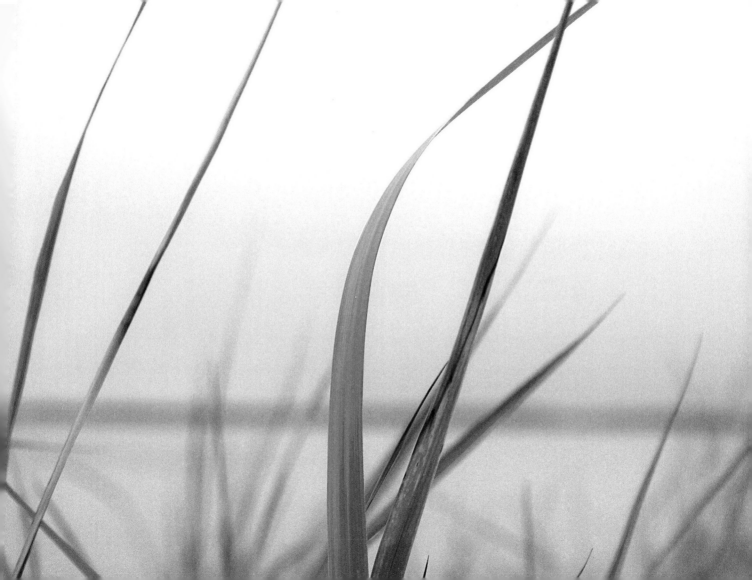

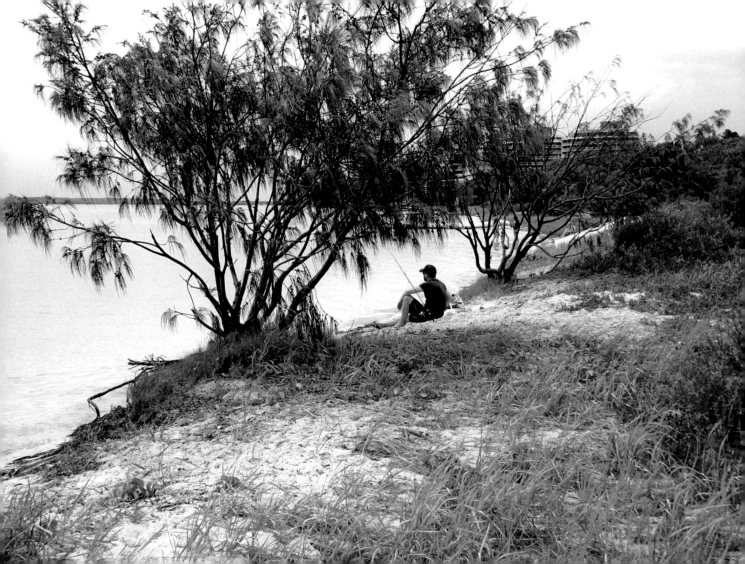

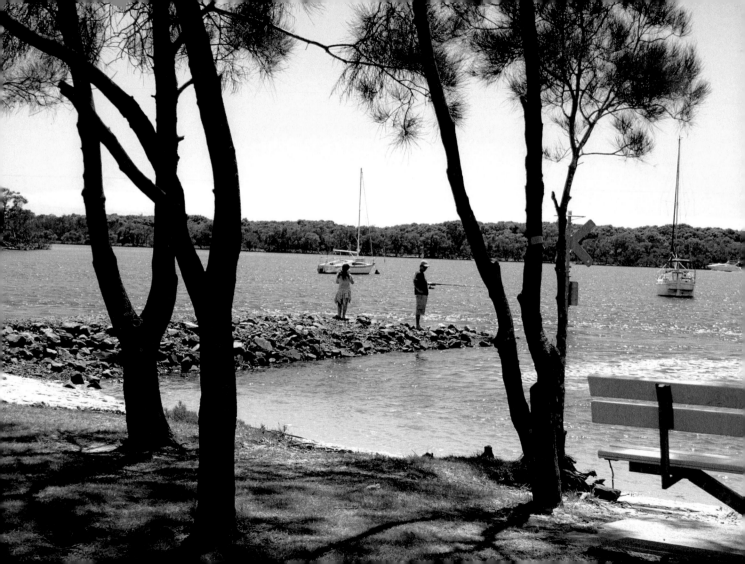

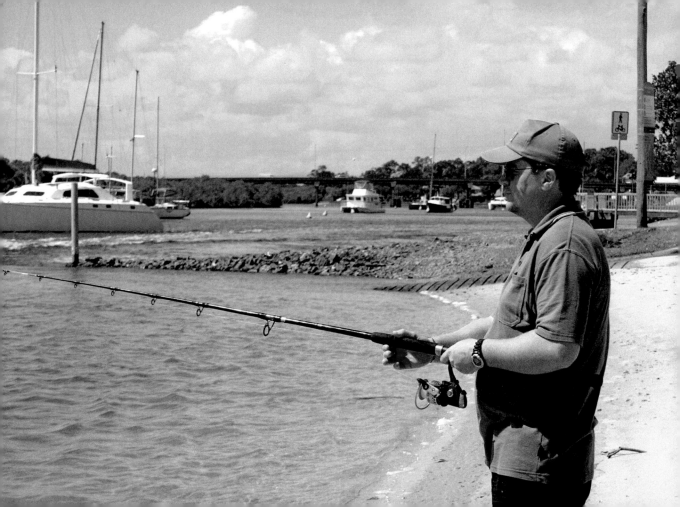

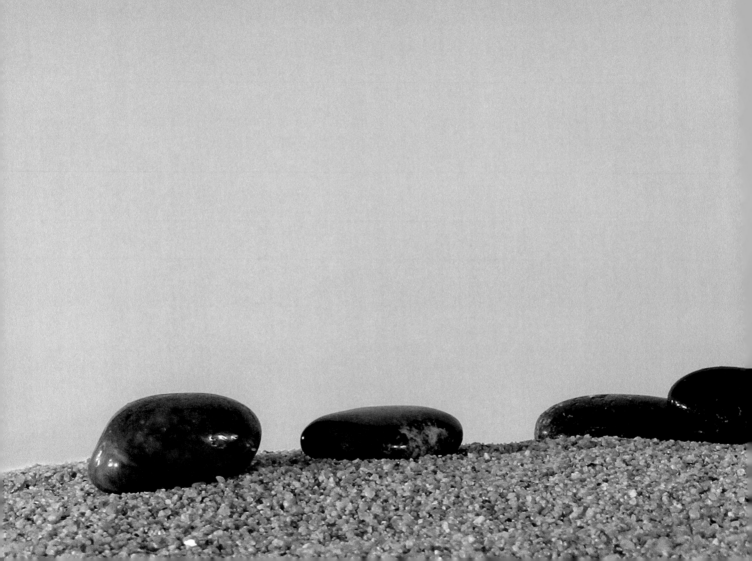

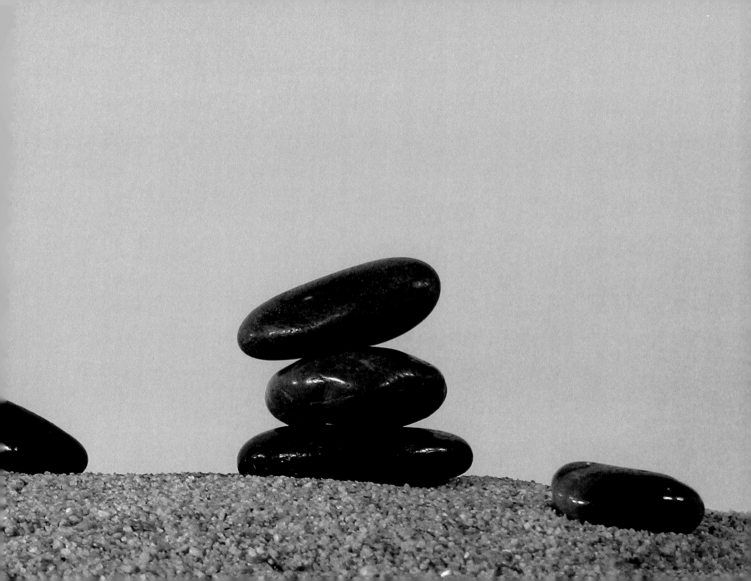

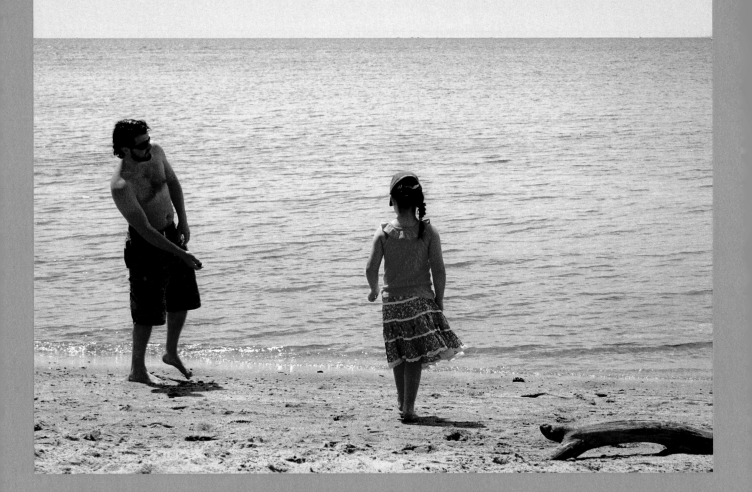

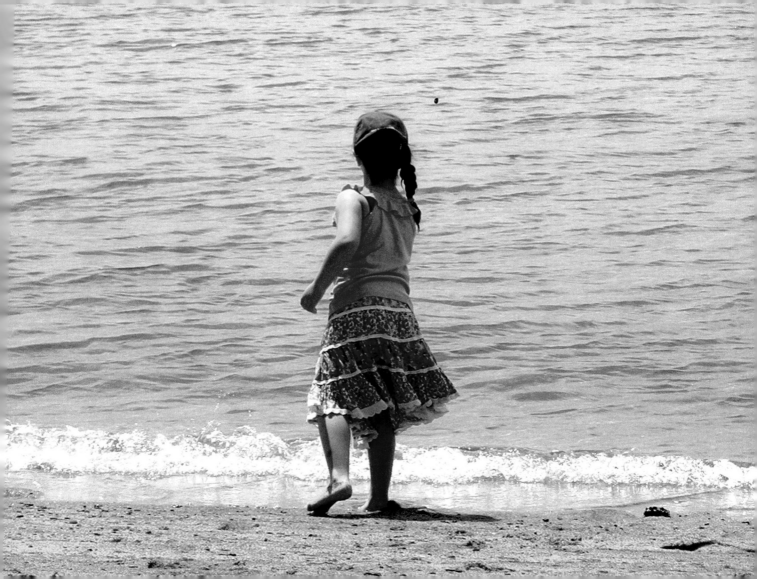

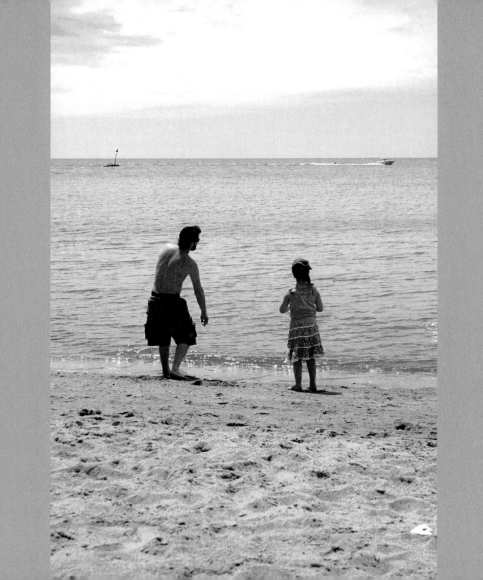

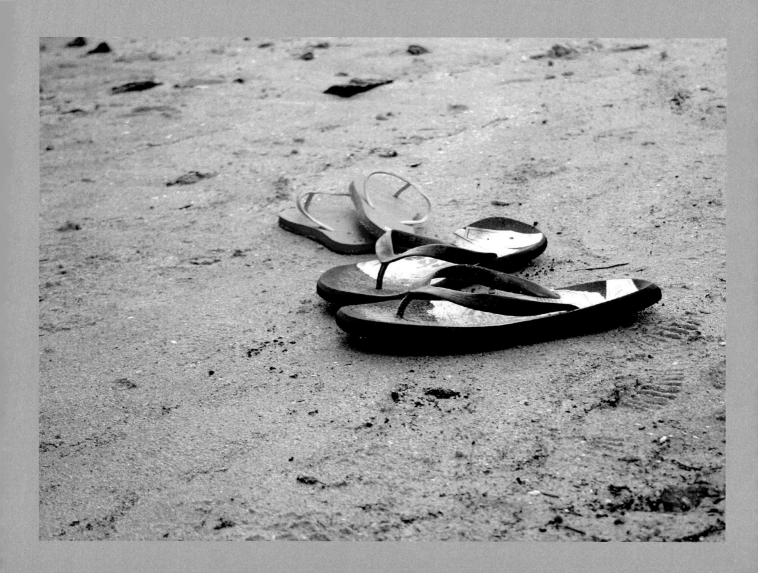

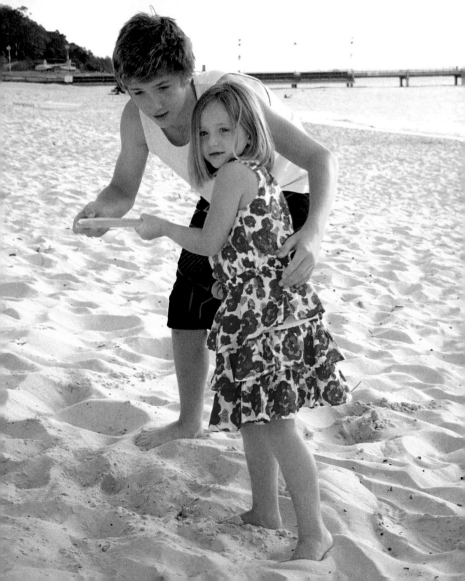

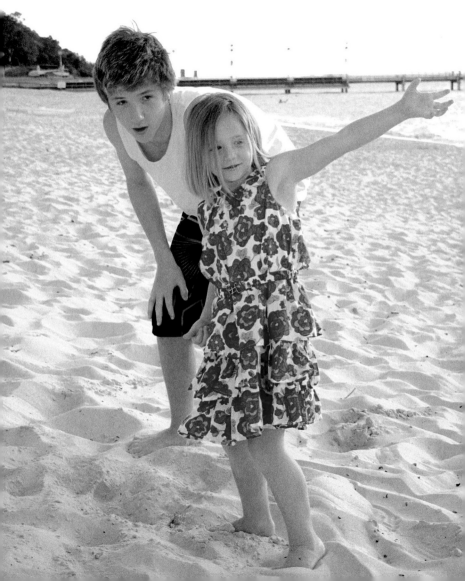

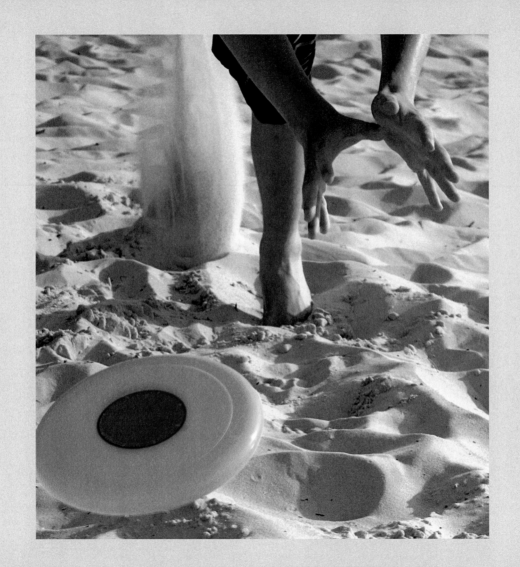

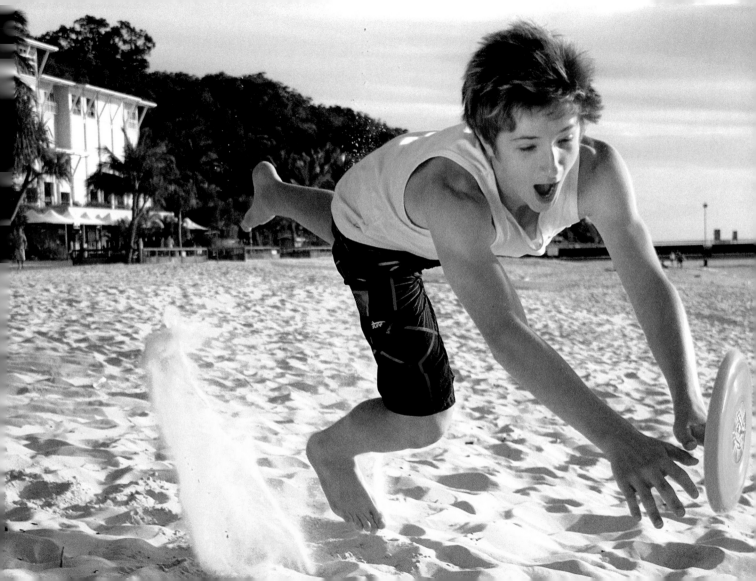

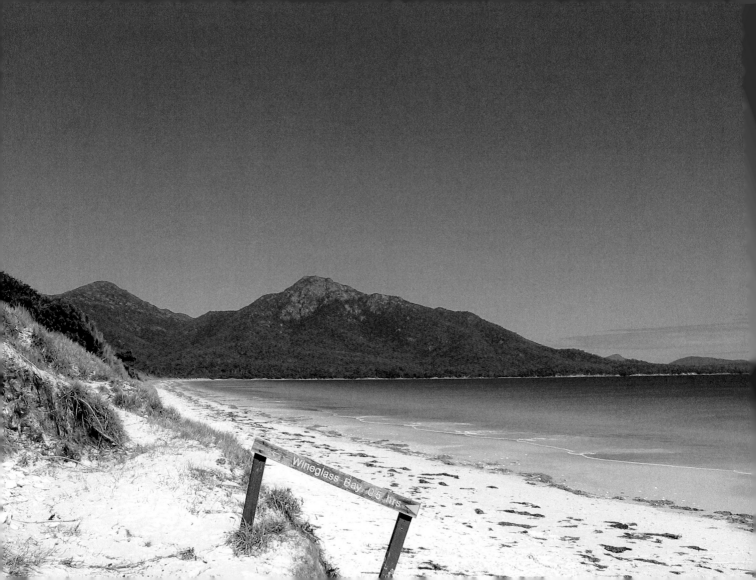

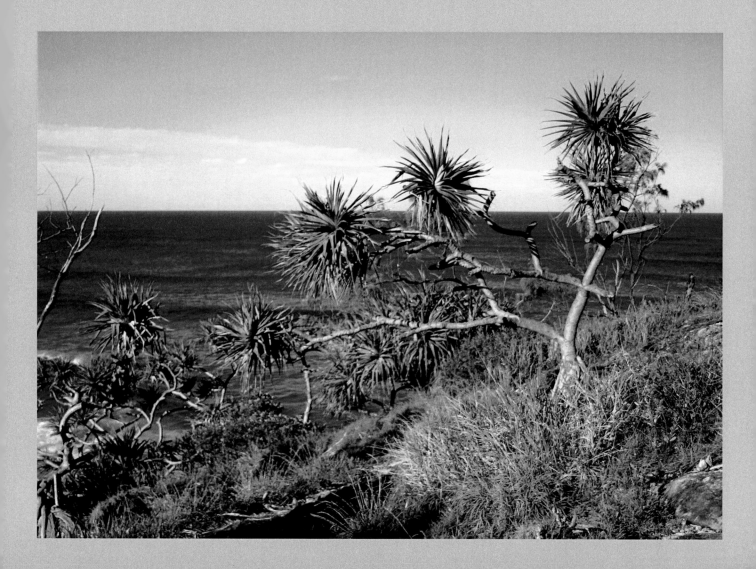

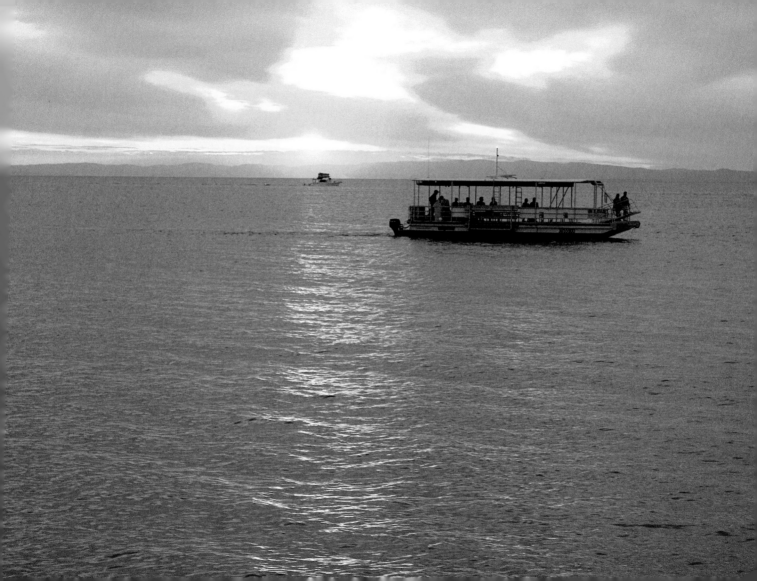

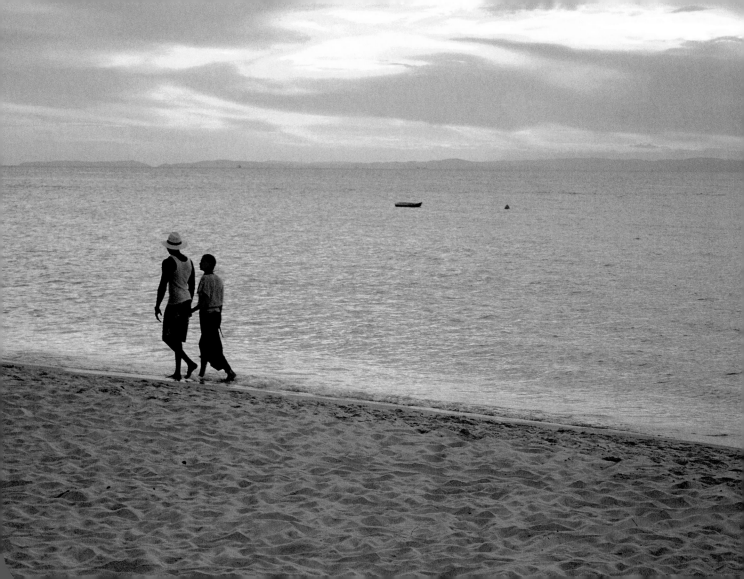